SCIENCE IN OUR WORLD

INDEX
GLOSSARY
& ACTIVITIES

to volumes 1 to 15

Grolier Educational Corporation

SHERMAN TURNPIKE, DANBURY, CONNECTICUT 06816

Editorial
Brian Knapp, BSc, PhD
Art Director
Duncan McCrae, BSc
Production controller
Gillian Gatehouse
Print consultants
Landmark Production Consultants Ltd
Printed and bound in Hong Kong
Designed and produced by
EARTHSCAPE EDITIONS

First published in the USA in 1991 by
GROLIER EDUCATIONAL CORPORATION,
Sherman Turnpike, Danbury, CT 06816

Library of Congress #91–075970

Cataloging information may be obtained
directly from Grolier Educational Corp.

ISBN 0-7172-7384-9

Contents

Using the master index

These are the 16 volumes that make up the Science in our World series:

1:	Weather
2:	Flights
3:	Sounds and Music
4:	Water
5:	Falling
6:	Light
7:	Don't throw it away!
8:	Electricity and Magnetism
9:	Food
10:	Senses
11:	Shapes and Structures
12:	How things work
13:	Fibers
14:	Woodland life
15:	Growing and Changing
16:	Index

Example index entry:

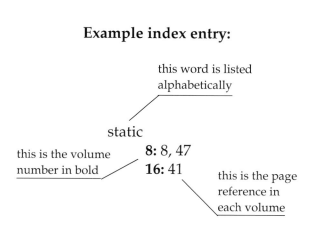

this word is listed alphabetically

static

this is the volume number in bold   **8:** 8, 47

            16: 41   this is the page reference in each volume

Index

A

absorb
    3: 18, 23, 46
    4: 34, 46
    11: 29, 46
    16: 21
absorbent **13:** 21, 32
ache **10:** 20
acid rain
    8: 43, 46
    16: 21
acorn **14:** 10, 11
aerosol
    7: 28
    12: 20, 21, 46
    16: 21
Africa
    1: 9
    9: 9
ailerons
    2: 29
    16: 21
air **8:** 13
air flow **2:** 11
airplane **2:** 28-9, 32-3, 36-7
air plant **1:** 15
air traffic control **2:** 38
airship **2:** 33
albatross **2:** 27
Alcock and Brown **2:** 33
algae
    14: 13, 35, 46
    16: 21
aluminum **7:** 32, 33
Amazon **1:** 24
amplifier
    3: 12, 26, 42, 46
    16: 21

anemometer **1:** 12
animal products **9:** 16
animals **7:** 13
annual plants
    7: 36, 46
    16: 21
Antarctic
    1: 9, 24
    4: 5
antennae
    10: 13, 18, 46
    16: 21
appliance
    7: 27, 46
    8: 6, 14, 17, 20, 46
    16: 21
arc
    5: 15, 18, 24, 46
    16: 21
arch **11:** 15
argon
    12: 34, 46
    16: 22
artificial light **6:** 8-9
asteroids **5:** 40
astronaut
    5: 9, 44-5
    13: 36
athletics **5:** 36
atmosphere
    1: 5, 8, 46
    6: 7, 46
    16: 22
aurora **8:** 44
Australasia
    1: 25, 36
    9: 9
autogyro
    2: 21, 46
    16: 22
automatic pilot **2:** 39
automatic reaction **10:** 42
autumn **14:** 42

avalanche
    5: 33, 46
    16: 22
average
    15: 12, 13, 14, 15, 46
    16: 22
avocado **9:** 21
ax
    5: 10
    12: 8

B

baby **15:** 6, 7, 8, 20
bacteria
    7: 43, 45, 46
    14: 9, 32, 46
    15: 17, 46
    16: 22
bagpipes
    3: 34, 35, 46
    16: 22
balance
    5: 14, 20
    10: 40
Bald Eagle **2:** 27
balding
    15: 25, 46
    16: 22
ball
    5: 12, 37
    11: 30
ball-point pen **12:** 15
ballet dancer **10:** 41
balloon
    2: 8
    8: 8
bamboo **11:** 11, 35
bananas **9:** 9, 26, 30
bang **3:** 7
banking **2:** 29
bar **11:** 18
bark **14:** 44

M

W

X

Y

Z

Glossary

absorb
to soak up
   shocks: rubber is an example of a material that changes shape and absorbs pulls and pushes
   sound: some of the best absorbing materials are those with rough surfaces or those with holes
   gas or a liquid: many powders absorb water and this causes them to swell

acid rain
when fossil fuels such as coal, oil and gas are burned in power stations and in car engines large amounts of a gas called sulphur dioxide are produced. This gas drifts up into the air and mixes with water droplets in the clouds. The raindrops that fall are acid. Acid rain can kill trees and the fish in lakes

aerosol
an aerosol is a mixture of small particles, such as water or paint droplets, suspended in a gas such as air. In a spray can the liquid that is to be made into particles is held under pressure with a gas. In the past the gases used were called CFCs. These gases are known to damage the environment.
   Aerosol cans now have different gases in them, but a hand cranked spray will do many of the jobs that a pressure can will do and it does no damage to the environment because it uses air to force the liquid through the nozzle

ailerons
in airplanes these are the flaps that can be lifted from the trailing side of the main wings. They are the flaps you see in use if you travel by air and look from the cabin windows. Pilots use them for changing direction and also for slowing the plane as it comes in to land

algae
tiny plants which grow together and make bright green, powdery patches on damp rocks and tree trunks

amplifier
something which makes sounds louder

annual (plant)
a plant that grows, flowers, sets seed and dies in a year

antennae
the main sensing organ of an insect. There are usually one or two pairs of antennae attached to the animal's head and they contain the receptors for sound, smell, touch and temperature

appliance
the name given to any electrical equipment used in the home, for example a washing machine or a stove. It could also mean a radio or TV

arc
a small part of a circle

argon
argon is a gas that makes up about one per cent of the air. It is called an inert gas, which means that it will not react with other substances easily. Argon is used in light bulbs or fluorescent lamps because it will not burn up when hot

atmosphere
the layer of gases around the Earth. The lowest part of the atmosphere includes enough oxygen for us to breath. It also holds large amounts of dust and other tiny particles that have been swept off the land by winds. Clouds only form in the lowest part of the atmosphere

autogiro
this is a machine that has freely spinning rotor blades. It is driven forward by a propeller. The forward movement of the machine causes the rotor blades to turn and this gives lift. It is not as maneuverable as a helicopter

avalanche
the rapid movement of a huge mass of snow down a mountainside. Avalanches can reach speeds up to hundreds of miles an hour and they can cause great damage to any buildings that lie in their paths

average
the word used to describe a value that is thought to be normal. The average is calculated, for example, by adding all the heights of a group together and then dividing by the number in the group

bacteria
microscopic organisms which are neither plant nor animal. Many kinds feed on the dead bodies of plants and animals. In even a handful of woodland soil there would be many millions of bacteria, all doing the useful job of helping to decompose dead material. As they do this they release gases

bagpipes
a musical reed instrument that is pumped with air supplied from an animal bladder

balding
the gradual loss of hair from the head because the hair producing cells in the scalp begin to die. It is a common feature of men, but very rare in women

barometer
an instrument for measuring the pressure of the air in the atmosphere. High pressure spells fine weather, low pressure forecasts rain, very low pressure tells of an approaching storm

bearing
a support for a moving part. The hub of a bicycle wheel contains a bearing. This allows the wheel to turn easily on the shaft

beat
a sound made regularly. The beat helps to maintain the rhythm and keeps the musical time

blizzard
a snowstorm with very strong winds. In a blizzard it is almost impossible to see ahead because of the driving snow

blood vessels

the tubes that carry blood from the heart to the rest of the body and back again. Blood is red when it has plenty of oxygen

bow (musical)

an instrument used for making strings vibrate. Bows only work if they are coated with rosin and make rapid juddering movements

brass (musical)

musical instruments played by the mouth using the lips as a reed

breeze

a gentle movement of air too light to rustle the pages of an open book

bricks

a special form of clay building block found widely in the world. Some bricks have specially shaped dents in their faces to take cement, others have plain faces. Bricks are about a quarter the size of concrete building blocks

bugle

a kind of simple horn designed for playing military tunes

camouflage

a pattern of colors designed to blend in with the surroundings. Most types of camouflage involve patterns of colors, such as stripes or blotches

animals: any way in which an animal makes itself difficult to be seen. Many animals have colors which let their body blend in with their surroundings. Green is a useful camouflage color for a caterpillar on a young leaf; speckled brown will camouflage an insect on the bark of a tree

canopy

the part of the wood above your head which is made by the interlocking branches of trees that are growing close together

carbohydrate

a group of substances that includes a number of sugar-making chemicals, of which the most important is starch

carding

the process which gets the natural fibers pulled out into line, removes the seeds and other small pieces of unwanted material

carnivore

an animal that eats mainly meat. Animals such as tigers, bears, or foxes are large carnivores, but a centipede, which eats other insects, is also a carnivore

cartilage

the rubbery layer of tissue - often known as gristle - that grows between moving bones and which acts as a combined bearing and shock-absorber

cell

shape: a closed shape that packs together with other similar shapes to form a pattern. In a honeycomb made by bees each cell is made of wax and is occupied by an egg

living: our bodies are made of millions of small building blocks called cells. Cells contain all the information necessary for life. The simplest organisms, such as bacteria, are each made of a single cell. Cells have evolved to perform many special functions, such as turning food into energy, or receiving signals about the outside world. Our bodies are constantly making new cells to replace the dead ones

cellulose
a natural material that makes up the bulk of plant tissues. Cellulose often forms into tiny strings, or fibers

center of gravity
it is often useful to try to work out the place where the real weight of an object lies. The term center of gravity is used to describe this place. If the object has most of its weight high up, it is probably 'top heavy'. It has its center of gravity high up. If the weight is mostly low down, it is 'bottom heavy' with a center of gravity low down. This position makes an object much less likely to fall over

centrifugal force
when an object whirls around and around it always tries to fly outwards and away from its orbit. Many people call the effect the centrifugal force

ceramic
a special kind of clay that has been baked hard. Most kitchen tiles are ceramic. Ceramics are hard and brittle, but they can stand up to great heat and they are therefore useful on the outside of a space craft when it flies back through the Earth's atmosphere

charge
the amount of stored electrical energy present. People often speak of 'charging a battery'. What they mean is that they must replace the electrical energy that has been used. To do this they use a piece of equipment called a 'charger'

chord
the effect you get when you play three or more notes at the same time

chrysalis
the silken case made by a caterpillar as it prepares to turn into a butterfly

circuit
a circuit is made of a number of electrical devices connected up in such a way that electricity flows through them. A circuit can be simple, as in the case of a flashlight, where a battery and a bulb are connected through a switch, or it might be very complicated, such as in a computer when tens of thousands of connections are involved

cirrus
a wispy form of cloud that forms in a clear sky. Cirrus cloud is very high in the sky and made entirely of ice crystals

clay
the finest size of rock flour produced when rocks are broken down by the action of the weather. Clay is too small to be seen piece by piece. When moist, clay feels sticky

cloud
water droplets or ice crystals that form in the air above the ground

cloven
a name used to describe the hooves of deer which are slit into two

cocktail
a mixture of a range of different liquids

cocoon
the silken wrapping or case made by a caterpillar as it prepares to turn into a moth. The silkworm gradually wraps itself in silk by pushing out a long continuous thread from a special place on its body

combustible
a material that can burn is said to be combustible. Three conditions are needed for combustion: the material, a source of heating such as a match, and a supply of air

concave
the way a surface is dished so that it faces inwards. Typical concave objects include the inside of a spoon and the inside of a cupped hand

condensation
the formation of water droplets on a cold surface

cone
a shape with a circular base and sloping sides that meet at a point. A wizard's hat is often shown as a tall cone in books

convection
this is a natural process that happens in a liquid or gas when they are heated or cooled. If a gas is made warmer it becomes lighter and starts to rise. If it gets cooler it becomes heavier and sinks. Air in contact with a heater rises as it warms. New air flows in to take its place and is warmed in turn. This sets up a flow of air or a current

convex
the way a surface is bulged out so that it faces outwards. The outside of a ball is a convex surface

co-ordination
the process of doing many linked things at the same time. For example, when we walk we normally co-ordinate the movement of our arms and legs to keep our bodies balanced

corrugation
a surface that is shaped into long lines of wrinkles. Corrugations are often added to materials to make them stronger. Sheets of wrapping paper and sheets of steel (intended for use as roofing) are common examples

counterbalance
when an object is balanced there must be the same weight on both sides of the pivoting point. A counterbalance is a weight that is added to a machine to get it into balance. Counterbalances are found in many places. They could be found as a weight on the end of a bar, or a weight on the end of a pulley

cumulonimbus
tall rain-bearing thunderclouds

cumulus
pillow-like clouds that can give showery weather

cyclone
a name given to a tropical storm with severe winds

cylinder
a solid shape with a circular plan. Rods, columns and trees are all examples of cylinders. A hollow cylinder is called a tube

decibel
a unit that gives a measure of the loudness of a sound

deciduous
when plants shed their leaves for part of the year and stop growing they are said to be deciduous. Many trees are deciduous to allow them to survive a harsh winter or a drought

decomposers
living things such as bacteria, fungi and earthworms which feed on the dead bodies of plants and animals and break them down, releasing materials that can be directly used as food by growing plants

detergent
a chemical that acts on surface grease to remove it. Many detergents are made of lots of chemicals that can dissolve most forms of dirt and grease

dew
condensation that forms on leaves and other surfaces overnight

diet
the types of food we eat. When people speak of 'going on a diet', they usually mean they are going to change their diet to one with less energy in it

digestion
the way in which the body breaks down the food into useful chemicals

dilate
a word that means to make larger. The pupil in the eye gets larger, or dilates, under dark conditions. This is done to capture the greatest amount of light possible and help an animal to see better

dimmer
a piece of electrical equipment that cuts down the voltage that reaches a light bulb.
   With less voltage (pressure) the bulb then glows less brightly and uses less electric current

disposable
an object or appliance that cannot be repaired once it has worn out or become broken. Many of the components of electronic machines such as computers use disposable parts, but most ball point pens cannot be refilled and these are therefore also disposable

dissolve
the way in which a solid is absorbed by a liquid. Water can dissolve more substances than any other liquid. Many substances are colorless when they have dissolved in water.
   smell: many small particles, or molecules, are in the air as it is breathed into the nose. As they

dissolve in the mucus of the nose the particles cause a chemical change and this sends signals to the brain

down
the very soft underfeathers of a bird. Chicks start life covered with down, but as they grow older the larger body and flight feathers grow through the down and hide it

drizzle
a form of light rain with small drops

drought
a period which is dry for longer than usual and when people, plants or animals start to suffer

drum
A sound box with a skin stretched across it. It is hit with the hand or sticks

dye
a staining or coloring chemical. Natural dyes have been used for thousands of years, but it is difficult to get a complete range of colors. Artificial, or synthetic, dyes are often made from oil

ear muffs
special 'headphones' that have sound deadening material inside each ear cup

eardrum
The flap of skin inside the ear that acts as a sounding board for vibrations in the air. As sound waves make it vibrate, so the bones inside the ear are also made to vibrate, thereby passing on the sound. The eardrum also serves as a door in the ear, keeping out dirt and liquids

earthquake
violent shaking of the ground due to great movements deep within the Earth. An earthquake can cause enough damage to buildings to make them collapse

echoes
the indirect sound we hear when vibrations are bounced from an object

eclipse
an eclipse occurs when one planet or Moon shuts out the direct sunlight to another. In an eclipse of the Sun, the Moon passes between the Sun and the Earth, almost blocking it out for several minutes

electromagnet
a form of temporary magnetism produced whenever an electric current flows in a wire. Temporary magnetism is very useful for operating switches by remote control

elevators (airplane)
these are small flaps in the tail of an airplane. Even small changes in the tail, will make a big change in direction of the airplane. This is why both the elevators and the rudder controls are placed in the tail

embryo
the word used to describe any animal or plant in the first stages of life, before it develops its final form

energy
the amount of effort needed to get something done
> **chemical**: the power in food locked away as chemicals. We release the energy during digestion;

electrical: the electrical power that is available to make appliances work;

light: the energy in light waves that plants can use to grow

equator

the line that divides the Earth equally in two and is half way between the poles.

evaporation

the way water changes from droplets to vapor

fabric

a cloth made from fibers by knitting, weaving, felting and a variety of other processes

fat

the substance that the body makes to store energy

felting

a special process of matting wool, cotton and other materials so they make a dense waterproof material. Felting is done using both heat and pressure

ferment

the process of rotting through the action of bacteria and fungi

fertilize

the process of bringing female and male parts together in order to produce new life. When fertilization takes place in a flower the contents of the pollen grain join with the contents inside the flower to make a seed

fiber

a natural or synthetic strand, or filament, of material

material: materials that may be spun into a thread. There are many fibers that are used in fabrics, from the thin strands of glass that make fiber-glass to the delicate fibers off sheep and goats that make wool

food: materials that are found in plants but which are indigestible

filament

the fine wire that is used in light bulbs. The wire is made of a special metal that will not easily melt even when it becomes white hot. Because the metal would burn away in air, a filament is placed in a glass bulb with a gas called argon

fleece

the coat of wool that covers a sheep or goat. The wool is not naturally straight, but has a natural crinkly shape which stands up even after it has become wet. A fleece is also covered with natural oils to help keep the hairs waterproof

fluorescent

a special property of some materials such that they give off light which we can see when they are put in a beam of light rays outside our normal range of vision. Fluorescent tubes use four or five times less energy than an ordinary bulb for the same light output

flute

a woodwind instrument without a mouthpiece. Sound is made by blowing across a mouth hole

fog
cloud at ground level. In a fog there are so many water droplets that it is impossible to see more than a few tens of feet

food chain
the many animals and plants that live together in a balance, each dependent on the other in some way

force
The effort that is applied on an object. There are many different ways of creating a force. Pushing this book so that it moves is an example of a force

fossil fuel
the fuels such as oil, coal and gas that are obtained from under the surface of the Earth

friction
the resisting force that builds up between two objects when one of them is subject to a force such as turning or pushing. There is a limit to the friction that can oppose movement

frond
the feathery leaf of a fern. On the underside can often be found brown spots which release spores

frost
air or ground temperature that falls below 32°F (0°C)

frostbite
when it is very cold, the blood vessels in the skin get smaller. Under extreme conditions, the blood vessels may get so small that they stop blood from carrying oxygen to the skin and the cells begin to die

fungi
a primitive kind of plant that does not bear flowers or develop proper seeds, but which distributes spores. Mushrooms and many molds are fungi. They cause dead tissue to rot

fur
the coat of fine hairs that cover many animals such as cats and dogs. Fur has the same purpose as the fleece of a sheep; it helps to keep the animal warm and dry

fuselage
the name given to the body of the airplane. The fuselage is usually cigar-shaped and it is braced to take the weight of the wings and tail

gale
wind that is severe enough to capsize small boats

gamelan
an Asian (Indonesian) orchestra which consists mainly of xylophone-type instruments and bells

gas
a substance that is a vapor. Many gases, such as oxygen, are invisible. The main gases of the air are nitrogen, hydrogen and oxygen

gastric juices
the chemicals the body makes in order to break down the food we eat

germinated
when seeds sprout into life they are said to have germinated

geyser
a natural fountain of hot water that spurts from underground. The name comes from Geysir, a hot fountain in Iceland. Geysers are found near to places where volcanoes have been active

gills
these are the special structures that allow fish and some other animals to absorb oxygen out of the water. Gills do the same job as lungs in land animals

glands
a group of cells which have become specialized for the purpose of producing some special chemical made from parts of the blood. Glands include those for releasing saliva in the mouth, sweat from the skin, and digestive juices inside the gut

gravity
this is the force produced by every object in the Universe. The force of gravity depends on the size of the object. If the object is the size of a marble, the gravity force it has is too tiny to notice. But when the object is the size of a planet, its force of gravity force is huge. Many animals make use of gravity to give them a sense of balance

greenhouse effect
when fossil fuels such as coal, oil and gas are burned they release a gas called carbon dioxide. This gas occurs naturally in the air, but the amount has doubled this century due to fuel burning. Carbon dioxide traps heat and makes the atmosphere warmer. The way it works is often said to be similar to the way a greenhouse warms up, so people call it the greenhouse effect

grid
a network of cables that allow power stations to be linked to homes. A grid allows electricity to be shared, so the power can be sent to wherever it is needed. The tall utility poles crossing the countryside carry cables that are part of the power grid

hail
a mixture of ice and water in the form of a ball-shaped lump. Hailstones only fall from thunderstorms

hardwood
hardwood trees have trunks with very closely packed fibers. This makes the wood dense and hard. Hardwoods are particularly useful for furniture and buildings because they do not easily rot or take up water. Hardwood trees grow very slowly and they are therefore hard to replace

harp
a string instrument held upright while the strings are plucked

harpsichord
a piano-like keyboard instrument where the strings are plucked

herbivore

an animal, such as a cow, a rabbit or an elephant, that gets all of its food needs from plants. People are not herbivores because they can choose to eat meat or plants. People fall into the group called omnivores

hibernate

a period of winter rest in an animal's life. During this time the animal is almost completely inactive. It breathes just fast enough to keep it alive

hormone

A hormone is a chemical messenger which is made in a special gland. There are glands scattered all over the body. However, some glands in women and men are different and this is what causes them to develop differently as they become grown-ups

horn

a tube-like instrument. It was originally a hollowed-out animal horn

hurricane

a word for a tropical storm

hydroelectric

a term meaning water-driven. Hydroelectric power is obtained by damming water in a reservoir and then releasing it in a tunnel. Inside the tunnel is a wheel called a turbine, that is turned by the rushing water. The wheel turns the shaft of a generator which in turn makes electricity

image

when light rays are bounced off a mirror, or bent through a lens, they show a picture of the objects they 'see'. This picture is called an image

incandescent

the light that is produced when a solid, such as a wire in a lamp, is heated

incisor

these are the sharp, chisel-shaped teeth at the front of the mouth. Their job is to cut into the food so that pieces can be torn off

ingredients

the foods that go to make up a mixture. The ingredients of a cake, for example, may be flour, water, fat, salt and cherries

insulate

an insulation is a covering of material that is designed to keep heat or electricity in or out. Insulation is used in the walls of many houses to keep them at a more even temperature, and to save the energy that would be needed for either heating or air conditioning. Plastic insulation is used to protect electrical cables

jet engine

this is a form of engine which works by igniting an explosive mixture of air and kerosene (a form of gasoline). The process is similar to the way a car engine works, but the exhaust gases are used directly to drive the airplane through the air. Jet engines work best at high altitudes, which is one reason airplanes fly as high as possible, often at about 42 000 feet

kaleidoscope
the name given to a toy that uses several mirrors all facing inwards. The kaleidoscope produces many images of any object placed inside and this may give many new patterns

key stones
the center stone of an arch made of blocks. Key stones are wedge-shaped so that they will fit around a curve

landfill
the name give to garbage that is dumped in an open pit, such as a disused quarry

larva (plural larvae)
the early stage in the life of many insects. Caterpillars are the larvae of moths and butterflies. Grubs are the larvae of beetles and flies

lens
when light passes through any transparent object that has curved sides the rays of light will be bent. The curved material is then a lens. A lens is used to change the size of things we look at. There are two common types of lens. In the kind called convex, the lens magnifies. You can recognise it because it has bulging sides. In the type of lens called concave the lens makes things smaller. This lens has dished sides

lever
this is a long bar which is used to help people to make light work of moving a heavy object. The lever is used with a pivot. The lever is placed under the heavy weight and over the pivot. The weight is lifted by pressing down on the other end of the lever

lift (in flight)
the force that carries a flying object upwards when it moves through the air quickly. It was discovered by an Italian scientist named Bernoulli. He found that a wing split the air in a special way as it went fast through the air and that this difference caused the wing to lift upwards

light
a special form of energy that can be seen. Light energy can travel through space, which is why the Sun can still give energy to our world even though the Sun and Earth are over 93 million miles apart

lightning
the spark that occurs when electricity passes from a cloud to the ground or between layers in a cloud. Fork lightning occurs when you see the spark; sheet lightning is the reflection of the spark

luminous
a material that glows when certain types of light shine on it, or which gives out light because of the way magnetism affects it

magnet
a material is magnetic when it has the ability to attract iron objects to it. Magnets have places where their magnetic effect is concentrated called magnetic poles. In a magnetic catch the pole of a magnet is placed so that it faces the strip of iron on the door

mammal
an animal that gives birth to live offspring (as opposed to, for example, laying eggs). People are mammals, as are deer, squirrels and many other warm-blooded animals with a skeleton of bone, a skin with hairs and which are raised on milk when they are very young

manufactured goods
any objects that have been made by machine. Most manufactured goods are designed to be easy to make and to assemble. Normally they are a mixture of several types of materials. This makes them very difficult to recycle

mass
this is the amount of matter in an object. Scientists use the word mass to talk about the amount of matter in an object because its weight changes with the force of gravity. A ball has the same mass on the Earth and on the Moon, but its weight will be much greater on the Earth where gravity is stronger. The mass of an object is measured in units called pounds

mature
a word used to describe when a plant or animal has grown to its full size

meanders
the regular twists and turns of a river. Most meanders are formed on the flat land at the bottom of a valley

mesh
the name given to the size of holes left when a net is made. The size of the mesh is very important in fishing nets, for example, because a big or coarse mesh allows small fish to escape and continue to grow

metamorphosis
a complete change that happens to an animal as it grows up to be an adult. The word metamorphosis is used only for dramatic changes such as caterpillar to insect or tadpole to frog

meteorite
these are pieces of rock that are scattered in space. It was pieces of rock like meteorites that originally made up the planets in the Solar system. The Earth draws meteorites towards it all the time. Most of them weigh just a few pounds and they burn up in the atmosphere to give shooting stars. It is rare for a meteorite to land on Earth

microbes
a general term used in this book for all microscopic organisms that may cause harm if they are left to multiply in food

microscopic
very tiny, needing a microscope to be seen clearly. Many receptors, such as the cells used for touch, taste and sight, are microscopic in size, but they can still provide large amounts of information for the brain

migration
this is the seasonal movement of animal populations between one region and another, usually connected with seasonal changes of climate or the animal's breeding cycle. A bird called the Arctic Tern makes the incredible migration of 11 000 miles between its breeding grounds in the Arctic and the Antarctic

minerals
naturally occurring substances of the Earth, such as chalk and iron, that plants and animals absorb and use to build their tissues

mirror
most mirrors are made of glass with a layer of silver painted on to the back to give the reflecting surface

mist
a thin form of fog. Usually you can see for more than a hundred feet but you cannot see any distant object

moisture
the word for water vapor in the air

molars
the back teeth which are broad and designed to crush food. The ridges of the upper molars fit closely into the valleys of the lower molars. You can feel this close fit when you rub your teeth together

molecule
the smallest possible particles of a substance. Everything around us, including ourselves, is made of molecules

molt
a period when animals loose all, or a large part, of their coats or skin. Dogs molt by shedding many hairs, snakes molt by shedding their entire skin

mortar
a mixture of cement and sand and lime that makes a fine paste suitable for cementing building blocks together

musical scale
a series of notes arranged in order

nectar
a scented, sugary solution produced by many flowers and which attracts insects, birds or bats. As the animal sips the nectar it brushes against the flower, bringing in pollen to fertilize the plant and taking more pollen away to fertilize other plants

nerve
a nerve is a special kind of cell, part of which has become stretched out into the shape of a single long fiber. When a nerve cell is stimulated from outside, perhaps by pressure if it is a nerve in a finger, an electrical signal is generated in the nerve cell and passed by the fiber to the brain. The nerves that connect the eye to the brain are often called the optical nerves. Nerves are extremely sensitive and if touched directly can cause considerable pain

nocturnal animal
an animal that is active at night and which rests during the day

noise
any loud sound that is thought to be unpleasant

note
a single sound. Notes are often played together to make chords. Pleasing patterns of notes make music

nutrients
the special chemicals that are needed to help build new cells. Plants get their nutrients directly from the soil; animals get nutrients by eating plants or other animals. Nutrients include calcium (from milk), salt and iron (from dark-colored vegetables)

observatory
a place for the scientific study of space. The world's largest optical observatories are placed on high mountains well away from the pollution of cities so they can get the clearest possible view of space

octave
the gap between two notes, the upper one being twice as high as the lower

opaque
a material which appears solid and which cannot be seen through. Most objects are opaque

orbit
this is the path made by a body that whirls around a fixed point. A ball on the end of a string makes a circular orbit as it whirls round. Most satellites make a nearly circular orbit as they go around the Earth, although some orbit in an oval shape

ore
any rock that contains useful amounts of metal. Most metals are extracted from their ores by heating in a furnace

organism
a general name for any plant or animal. The word micro-organism is often used to describe the very large number of unseen living things that exist in water and which have no commonly used name

overloaded
a term meaning that more electrical current is flowing than the system can handle.
    At home an overloaded system will cause a fuse to blow

pan-pipes
South American bamboo pipes that are mounted in sets of differing lengths

parallel circuit
when electrical items such as bulbs are connected in parallel, each item is directly connected to the supply. The current flows from the negative terminal to the positive terminal through each item at the same time

percussion
the name for any instrument that makes a sound when it is struck

perennial
a plant that lives for many years

periscope
a device for reflecting light through two right angles. This makes it possible for an observer to see over obstacles or around corners

photosynthesis
the process that plants use to make new cells from sunlight, water, air and minerals in the soil

pier (building)

a thickened piece of a wall designed to give strength and to stop the wall from falling over

pile

the yarns of a fabric that stand up from the surface of the fabric. Velvet and carpets have a pile. In the case of carpets the pile is made by looping many yarns through a backing sheet

pitch (musical)

the name used to say how high or low the note is

pivot

a point about which an object can turn. For example the shaft and hub of a bicycle wheel is a pivot for the wheel. A door pivots about its hinges

placenta

a piece of special tissue that is attached to the inside of the womb. The baby is attached to the placenta by the umbilical cord

plaque

a substance produced in the mouth. It is a sticky acid substance that makes the food for bacteria. At the same time as eating the plaque, the bacteria eat into the surface of the teeth causing tooth decay. Toothpaste contains substances which balance out the acid and stop bacteria from feeding

pole (magnetic)

the name given to each end of a line. The Earth acts like a long magnet with its ends, or poles, near to the North Pole and the South Pole. As a result the magnetic poles are also called north and south. North and south poles are also used to describe the ends of all other magnets

pollen

A 'dust' made by the flower. Each grain of 'dust' is really a very tiny case containing a substance which is used to fertilize a flower and help make a seed

pollutant

a substance that fouls water. People use the word pollutant to mean the waste chemicals from factories, ships, homes and farms. Together these often spoil water and make it unhealthy and unpleasant

polyester

a range of synthetic fibers made originally from oil. Polyester fibers are very springy, so they will always try to spring back to their original straight shape. This is what makes polyesters resist creasing

polyp

an animal with a hollow cylindrical body with tentacles round the mouth. Many coral animals are polyps. They make a finned chalky frame as they grow. This remains after the animal has died and becomes a permanent part of a coral reef

pores

the surface of the skin has many tiny holes in it. These holes are called pores. Some pores allow fluids, such as sweat, to flow out, others – follicles – provide openings for growing hair

pot hole

pits that have been formed in the bed of a river by the swirling action of water and pebbles. As the pebbles go round and round in the pot hole, so they wear away the sides and also themselves

power

the rate at which electrical energy is fed into or taken out of a circuit. It is usually measured in watts

precipitation

any form of water or ice that falls from a cloud. It includes rain, hail, drizzle, snow and sleet

predator

any animal that kills and eats other animals. Foxes and some beetles are examples of predators

primary colors

the minimum number of colors that, when mixed in the right proportions, can give all the other colors of the spectrum. They are usually red, green and blue

printed circuit

this is a pattern of connections that are made in many pieces of electronic equipment. All the connecting wires are made of flat strips of metal which are stuck down onto a base board. Because they are fixed down there is less chance of mistaking the connections or of the wires breaking

prism (optical)

the name of a triangular-shaped piece of transparent material, usually glass. Its sides are frequently cut at an angle of 45 degrees. When light enters a prism it is turned back on itself. Prisms are used in binoculars to shorten the length of the sighting tubes. One special property of prisms is to show that white light is really made up of many colors

projectile

this is any object that is thrown or shot into the air. The projectile might be an arrow, a stone, a ball or a bullet. All make the same type of curving path as they fly through the air

protein

the name given to substances that make the walls of the bodies cells. Young people need to eat a large amount of protein otherwise their growth might be stunted

pulp

the name given to the mashed up fibers of wood or recycled paper. Most pulp made in a factory has been through many chemical stages to get it to an even texture and a desired color

pupa (plural pupae)

a stage in the life of many insects which is after the larval stage. At this time the insect is enclosed in a bullet-shaped case. Sometimes the pupa is called a chrysalis

pupil (eye)

the dark center to the eye. The size of the pupil is controlled by changes in the iris, the colored part of the eye

pyramid

a shape with a square base and four sloping triangular sides that meet in a point. The most famous examples of a pyramid are the Pyramids of Giza, huge burial chambers of the ancient Egyptian kings or pharaohs

quarry

any large pit in solid rock that has been made by people searching for resources in the ground. Chalk, stone and metal ore quarries make some of the world's largest sites for garbage

quartz

this is a common mineral that makes sand and glass. In its crystal form it is transparent

radar

the equipment used to find airplanes in the sky. A radio signal is sent out from a transmitter. When it reaches a plane or other solid object some of the waves are bounced back and detected by a receiver. The time it takes for the signal to go out and come back gives the position of the airplane

rapelling

is used by people when they want to get down a cliff very quickly. They make a series of jumps down the cliff, using the rope to support their weight. It is very important to use a rope with just the right amount of stretch or the rope might break

ray (light)

the path followed by light as it moves from its source. Light can be made into rays by putting an obstruction, such as a comb, in front of a beam of light

receptor

a special kind of nerve cell that turns a sense such as sight, taste, sound or touch, into an electrical signal which is sent to the brain. The receptor cells give the brain all of its information about the outside world. They also feed back information that help the brain to work organs such as limbs

reconditioned

a machine that has been reconditioned is one where the worn out parts have been replaced. Reconditioning equipment gives a new lease of life and is cheaper than replacing the whole machine

rectangle

a square shape with all sides at right angles. However, unlike squares, rectangles do not have all sides the same length. A square is a special form of a rectangle

rectangular

the name for the shape of any block-shaped object. All the angles in a rectangular block are right angles

recycle

recycling refers to the way people can reuse materials to make new and useful products from old and worn out ones

reed (musical)

a small piece of material that vibrates when air is blown across it

reserves

the amount of material left in the Earth and which can be extracted by pumping or mining. The amount of reserves often gets larger as people find new ways to extract the desired material

resin

this is a material rather like glue that comes from trees

retina

the part of the eye on which image is formed after light has passed through the lens. There are millions of tiny light-sensitive cells on the retina surface. Human eyes have both rods (which tell black from white) and cones (which tell about color). Each rod or cone is a nerve cell that is separately linked to the brain

rhythm

the way the music is set out in time

rod

any slim cylinder of material giving it a stick-like shape

rosin

special sticky material made from turpentine

rotor

the name given to the long thin blade set that is fitted to the helicopter. Rotors have special joints at their center which allow the pilot to change the angle of the blades

saline

Anything that has a lot of salt in it is called saline. Usually the word means that the water has so much salt that it is unfit to drink or will harm plants

saliva

the chemicals that are produced by salivary glands when you begin to eat. Saliva is a mixture of many substances designed to lubricate your food as it goes down your throat. At the same time the chemicals begin to break down, or digest, the food

sand

the smallest pieces of ground up rock that we can still easily see. Sand is commonly found on beaches, in deserts, and on the bed of rivers

sapling

a young tree. Saplings have supple stems and branches which can easily stand up straight again if they are knocked over. This natural springiness helps the young tree survive trampling by animals

satellite

a body that is trapped in a roughly circular path by the gravity of a larger body. The Earth and other planets are satellites of the Sun. The Moon is the Earth's largest satellite. Most satellites, however, are small machines sent into space to orbit the Earth

saxophone

a reed instrument with a curved and bell shaped end

scent

the smell or odor that is created when microscopic particles leave the scented object and become scattered in the air. When scent particles reach the nose they are dissolved in the mucus and turned into a chemical signal

shearing
a tearing type of action that happens when two blades close on a material like paper

skein
a length of yarn that has been wound into a long coil. Skeins are useful ways of storing yarns. Knitting wool is often sold in skeins

skyscraper
a building used as apartments or offices, which is unusually tall and which is made with a frame to hold it up

sleet
a partly melted form of snow

snow, snowflake
ice crystals that have formed into large groups to make a snowflake, and many snowflakes fall as snow

solar
a name give to the Sun. Solar energy is the light energy of the Sun. Plants use this energy to make their tissues. Scientists expect solar energy to become very important as a means of power for people in the next century

solution
The name given to describe the mixture of one substance inside another. A salt solution is made of water and salt, but if the water is boiled away, the salt will reform

sound
a sound is caused when there is a rapid disturbance in air. It may be produced in the throat to give speech or singing, or it may be due to some other movement such as a loudspeaker vibrating or a balloon exploding

sound barrier
the speed at which a flying object catches up with the sound waves that it produces. People have used the sound barrier as a goal when designing faster and faster planes. The sound barrier is reached at a speed of 1130 feet per second

sound box
a form of amplifier that is used to make musical instruments louder

space (astronomical)
the region beyond the Earth's atmosphere containing all the planets and stars. It is often used to mean the Universe except for the Earth

species
a group of plants or animals that can breed among its members. Oaks make a species because pollen from one oak tree can fertilise a flower from another oak

spectrum
the range of colors that make up white light

sphere
a ball-shaped object. Spheres roll easily in any direction and they are used in many bearings

spinning (fiber)
the process of twisting fibers of wool, cotton, hemp and other short fibers together so that they give a long thread or yarn which can then be used to make fabrics. Long fibers such as silk are not spun, but simply wound together to make threads

spore
a very tiny grain which contains part of a fungus, moss or fern. Spores will grow readily on damp ground

stall (flight)
this is the steepest angle that a wing can get lift. If the angle of the wing gets steeper the lift will disappear and the wing will no longer be able to keep the body in the air. Stalling can be a major cause of airplane crashes

staple
foods that are essential to healthy living. Staples include grains such as wheat, corn and rice

star
stars are balls of intensely hot liquid and gas. Our Sun is a small star compared with many in the Universe. Stars are so hot that no solid rock can form

starch
one of the common substances in the carbohydrate group. Starches are our most common form of day to day energy

static
a form of electric charge that builds up on the surface of some objects. If the charge gets big enough a spark can jump the gap. Lightning is caused this way

stereophonic
a system for recording and playing sound using two or more microphones and loudspeakers

stock (food)
a liquid made from boiling animal products such as bones with vegetable remains to get the remaining goodness from them

Stone Age
the earliest time of civilization, over 3000 years ago, when people mainly used stone implements

storm force wind
a wind that is so strong it can damage buildings as well as capsize ships at sea

stratus cloud
thick, heavy flat clouds, often with ragged rolls of cloud below. They belong to areas of low pressure and storms

streamline
a streamlined shape is one that has been shaped to give the least drag as an object moves. It is particularly important that fast moving objects, such as aircraft, are streamlined

supple
a material that is supple can bend easily without damage. The new shoots on a tree are very supple and will bend over on themselves without breaking, yet they can also stand up straight when no force is applied

surface tension
the way that some liquids such as water behave in the presence of air by having the appearance of an elastic skin. Surface tension keeps water droplets whole instead of spreading out as a film

synchronized
when many items all move in step they are said to be synchronized. Many actions of animals are synchronized, such as walking

tease
the process of gently pulling at a matted collection of fibers so they become loosened and then can be separated. Teasing is an essential first step in spinning

territory
the area that an animal tries to keep for its own use. Males will fight over territories because once they have mated, the territory must have enough food to support male, females and offspring

textile
the general name for any kind of fabric or cloth, but especially when it has been woven

thermal
the rising current of air that allows gliders and birds to get lift. Thermals are strongest on a clear day when the Sun can warm the ground. As some places warm faster than others the air above them warms fast as well. This warm air then becomes light and starts to float upwards, creating a thermal

thermometer
the instrument used to measure temperature. It is marked in degrees Celsius, shown as °C, for short or degrees Farenheit, shown as °F

thunder
the sound that is heard when a flash of lightning occurs. The thunder is made by the air as it is quickly heated by the lightning spark

transparent
a material which will allow light to pass through it. Glass and water are examples of transparent materials

treatment plant
A place for processing the polluted waters of rivers or waste-pipes. Treatment works use filters and microbes to get rid of the most poisonous substances. When water leaves a treatment plant it should be good enough to drink

tropics
the lands that lie on either side of the equator and where the Sun shines directly overhead at least once a year

trumpet
a brass wind instrument. The sounds are made by shaping the lips in a special way against the trumpet mouthpiece

turbine
A machine with many blades that is used to make electricity. Rushing water is used to turn the blades and these in turn cause the shaft of an electric generator to turn. The faster the water flows, the quicker the turbine turns and the more electricity is made

typhoon
a term for a tropical storm

ultrasounds
sound waves which are too high to be heard by the normal human ear. Some animals find ultrasounds particularly useful for getting a sense of direction and for finding food

ultraviolet light
this is part of the wide range of light that comes from the Sun. We can only see part of the Sun's radiation. This is called visible light. The type of radiation that is out of our visual range and just beyond violet is called ultraviolet

Universe
the Universe is the name for everything that we know to exist, the Earth, the Sun, and all the other stars, planets and space beyond them

vacuum
this is the absence of air. A vacuum exists in space but a near vacuum can be made for certain special reasons. The most common near vacuum is found in thermal bottles and in television tubes. If one of these containers is broken the air rushes in and gives the effect of an explosion, scattering pieces of sharp glass. It is therefore dangerous to break vacuum bottles

valve (musical)
a device which opens and closes over holes in wind instruments. There are many kinds of valve. Some are simple flaps over holes such as in the flute, whereas others are worked by pistons, such as in brass instruments

vein
the water channels in the leaves of plants. The veins are hollow tubes and so they help to strengthen the plant and make leaves stand stiff

vermin
any creature that may carry disease and which is seen as a pest. Very often it refers to rodents such as rats and mice

vibration
a regular pattern of movements. Sound waves are vibrations

violin
a string instrument played with a bow

vitamins
essential chemicals that the body uses to help prevent illness and in many other essential processes, They are easily destroyed by cooking or storing food. This is why fresh food is so essential

vocal chords
the part of the lower throat that has two flaps of skin that vibrate as air flows over them. The vocal chords are used with the mouth to form many types of sound

volume
the amount of space taken up by an object. Volume is measured by multiplying together the length, breadth and width of an object

water cycle

The never-ending way in which water moves around the world. People normally think of the cycle as starting in the oceans. They then follow the path of the water through clouds and rain, through rocks and soil, to the rivers that return the water to the sea

water repellent

A substance such as grease that will not dissolve in water. A water repellent painted on to a cloth will not let water get to the fibers. Many raincoats are treated with water repellents

water vapor

The kind of water that occurs as an invisible gas, and is often called 'moisture'. The amount of water vapor that can be held in the air gets less at lower temperatures, so a cold day forces much vapor to be turned back to water droplets. This gives dew

weather

the day to day nature of the air. Weather is measured by temperature, windiness, cloud, sunshine and moisture

weaving

the interlacing of threads or yarn to form an interlaced pattern that will not fall apart. This process is still done by hand in many countries, but it can also be done very swiftly by machine. A weaving frame was one of the first machines that started the industrial revolution over two hundred years ago

weed

a weed is a plant that will easily grow at a site but which a gardener or farmer does not want. Weeds are valuable in woodlands because they are quick to cover up a piece of bare ground

weight

objects have a weight due to gravity. A table tennis ball and a lump of lead of the same size will weigh different amounts because of gravity. The weight of an object is measured in units called Newtons

wind

the flow of air over the Earth's surface. Usually it is measured in feet per second

womb

the place inside the female's belly where the baby develops. The womb, or uterus, is a tube-like muscle which is strong enough to push the baby out when it is time to give birth

xylophone

a percussion instrument made of a row of tuned wooden or metal blocks that are hit with sticks

yarn

a continuous twisted strand of fibers produced by a process such as spinning

Activities